The 3 Proven Keys

That Instantly Unlock Profits

———————

Merle Liske

Published by Preeminent Press

THE 3 PROVEN KEYS THAT INSTATNLY UNLOCK PROFITS

Copyright © 2011 by Merle Liske

Published by Preeminent Press

ISBN 978-0-9878213-0-0

ABOUT THE AUTHOR

Merle Liske believes in a community that richly rewards its businesses that give more value than it receives from the people it serves. To achieve that vision, Merle founded a marketing and business growth consulting agency in Alberta, Canada where he is the managing consultant.

Merle prepares and executes custom marketing strategies tailored to the needs of his clients' unique requirements to help achieve their revenue goals. He draws on thousands of tactics used by businesses in hundreds of different industries to arrive at a unique strategy for each client.

Merle is a prolific author and is famous for achieving the status of **best selling author** on Amazon Kindle **twice in the same day** for two books on marketing in June 2013 with another paperback book due to be published in July 2013.

Merle is best known for teaching his clients that there are only three ways to grow a business:

1. attracting new clients

2. generating repeat clients

3. increasing the value of each client transaction

The strategies and tactics he employs for his clients target at least one of these three keys to growing a business. When all three are targeted, the results can be stellar. As Merle would tell you, "You want to increase your revenue by only 10%?! I won't do that but you can find someone on Craigslist that will take your money for a negative ROI. I only do 20% to 100% to 1000% or more... until you beg me to stop."

Merle Liske

Preeminent Business Systems Inc.
101-5101 50 Avenue
Suite 710
Leduc, AB
T9E 0B9
CANADA

780-665-4321(local/long distance)
800-576-6191(toll-free Canada/US)

Merle@PreeminentBusinessSystems.com

www.PreeminentBusinessSystems.com

CONTENTS

Chapter 3

Chapter 4

Chapter 5

Income Disclaimer

This book contains business strategies, marketing methods and other business advice that, despite my results and experience, may not produce the same results (or any results) for you. I make no guarantee, expressed or implied, that by following the advice within this book you will make any money or improve your current profits, as there are several factors and variables that come in to play with any proposed strategy.

Primarily, results will depend on the nature of the solution offered or business model used, the conditions of the marketplace, the experience of any individuals involved, and situational elements that are beyond our control.

As with any business endeavor, you assume all risk related to any investment based on your discretion and at your potential expense.

Liability Disclaimer

By reading this book, you assume all risks associated with using any advice provided, with a full understanding that you, solely, are responsible for anything that may occur as a result of putting this information into action in any way, and despite your interpretation of the advice provided.

You further agree that I cannot be held responsible at all for the success or failure of your business as a result of the information presented within this book. It is your responsibility to conduct your due diligence by paying attention to the safe and successful operation of your business if you intend to apply any of our information in any way to your business operations.

With that out of the way...let's continue with the exciting marketing strategies that successful businesses are using to increase their profits! But before we begin...

INTRODUCTION

20 COMMON MARKETING MISTAKES

From my experience, there are common mistakes that many businesses make; maybe yours included. Mistakes that are costing you money or unrealized profits. If you're guilty of enough of them over a long enough time your business is at risk of being added to the statistics of failed businesses.

Here they are in no particular order, common marketing mistakes:

1. Not testing all marketing ideas and variables.

2. Running institutional (look at me, here's what I got) instead of direct response advertising.

3. Not articulating and differentiating your business.

4. Not having a back-end product or service.

5. Not understanding your customers and prospects needs and desires.

6. Cutting prices instead of educating the market why they should pay your prices.

7. Not making doing business with you easy, appealing and fun or comfortable.

8. Not telling you're target market why to do business with you.

9. Terminating marketing campaigns that are still working.

10. Not being specific when targeting your marketing.

11. Not capturing prospects contact information.

12. Not being strategic and focusing on tactics.

13. Not having an integrated marketing or sales system.

14. Shooting from the hip in sales situations (fire, ready, aim).

15. Getting stuck doing things that work.

16. Not reinvesting profits.

17. Not knowing and leveraging the lifetime value of a customer.

18. Not analyzing and optimizing your assets, relationships, opportunities and resources.

19. Treating marketing and sales as separate operations silos.

20. Not taking advantage of integrating the Internet into every aspect of your marketing.

Can you identify with some of these? You are not along. Many businesses are struggling today not because of the economy or any other outside influence, rather, because they're committing many if not all of these mistakes. Correcting even one or two of these could make the difference between success or failure in your business.

I could write a book on every one of those mistakes and how to fix them, but the purpose of this book is to give you examples of strategies used by real businesses to get profitable results.

And of course, should you need any help implementing any of these tactics and integrating them into your existing marketing strategy, or overcoming any of your marketing mistakes, please don't hesitate to contact me by going to: www.PreeminentBusinessSystems.com and using the contact page or by dropping me an email at Merle@PreeminentBusinessSystems.com and I'll answer any questions, comments or concerns that you have with developing and accomplishing these powerful marketing strategies..

So, let's get started…

CHAPTER 1

PROVEN STRATEGIES FOR PROFITABLE RESULTS

This book might be the *'secret weapon'* your business has been waiting for to gain the competitive edge over your competitors, but you might be wondering...

Why I Created This Powerful Resource

Well the answer is simple: If I can <u>increase your sales,</u> using **just** these **FREE** strategies, I know you are going to be **even MORE excited** to see the *other* strategies I can implement to provide additional sales for your business!

However, another reason I wrote this book can be summed up with this quotation from B. C. Forbes:

"If you don't drive your business,
you will be driven out of business."

You see, by sharing this simple three-step system for increasing your profits…I know I can help you achieve the best results possible for skyrocketing your sales, which means you help more clients as well, creating a win-win result for all concerned!

According to the U. S. Small Business Administration more than **50% of small businesses fail within the first five years** of their operation. The principal reason for their failure can be linked back to one thing: *lack of an effective marketing strategy.*

Most businesses, especially in this economy, are struggling to attract new sales, and at a basic level, new clients, because they approach marketing the same way: *just putting out advertisements and **hoping** that their prospects see them and buy.*

However, successful businesses, the ones that are **dominating** in their markets, realize that a *powerful marketing plan* cannot only give them exposure to qualified prospects, but also allow them to increase their sales, and crush their competition, at a **fraction of the marketing expense** that their competitors are spending to attract fewer similar results!

Would such marketing results have a powerful impact on your sales numbers?

Would you be *excited* knowing you have a marketing advantage over your competition...especially as your sales increase as theirs *continue to decline*?

Would being able to drive more business, more sales, exposure to your business—despite the current economy—get your adrenaline pumping?

Well if you answered, 'Yes!' to the above questions then you now know...

Why This Book Has Everyone So Excited

Most businesses focus on just **one** way of increasing their sales: finding more prospective leads that eventually become paying clients.

However, there are **THREE** *ways to increase your business' sales*: generate more prospects, improving the sales closing percentage by turning potential buyers into paying clients, and, finally, increasing the value each client provides your business.

The three-step system in this book *not only* allows you to **obtain growth in all three areas**, but also as a result, you can generate a larger increase in sales because of the exponential combined growth in all three areas—making you unbeatable!

So with that said, now you just need to…

Read Through Each Strategy And Accomplish Them

If you have any questions, comments, or concerns about how to accomplish them, just ask me by using the contact information at PreeminentBusinessSystems.com and I can provide you with any additional information you need to get started, but now I recommend you start with…

CHAPTER 2

GETTING PROSPECTS EXCITED TO BUY FROM YOU

Let's face it, most of your competitors are taking a 'shotgun' style approach to their marketing—basically just spraying out as much advertising and marketing material as possible, while hoping the right person sees the advertisement and responds to it. An expensive approach that has a poor return on investment compared with...

Instead having a more laser-focused, and targeted, approach to getting your marketing messages in front of only those highly qualified prospects ready to buy the solution you are offering, which can be accomplished for a fraction of what your competition is spending on their marketing, especially when you...

Get Other Businesses To Happily Promote You To Their Clients

This is important because word-of-mouth recommendations are the best forms of marketing, and when you combine that recommendation with **an official endorsement** from a trusted company to their clients…you now have a <u>powerful</u> source of new leads to launch your sales to new levels.

Not only are these new leads much more open to the idea of buying from your business—as a result of receiving the trusted recommendation from a business they are dealing with—but they are also **highly qualified**, and precisely the ideal clients you want to generate from any 'traditional' advertisements.

For example, a personal development business in South Africa used the same strategy to **increase enrollment numbers into their seminars from 3.6% to an astounding 11%**—and they accomplished this for almost next to nothing!

How did they do this?

Well, after realizing for some time that their existing marketing methods were generating poor-quality leads, and with budgetary constraints because of recent changes in their business model, they decided to approach another local business—an Internet service provider with roughly 100,000 subscribers—who serviced the exact type of clients their personal development seminars were designed to help.

The personal development company then '*cut a deal*' with the ISP to provide free, two-hour lectures, to the clients of the ISP where they would educate, entertain, and inspire many people, then ultimately offer them the opportunity to buy a ticket to one of their coming, relatively expensive, seminars.

Then the ISP sent out an endorsement e-mail to their database of clients, inviting them to attend these free lectures '*as a means of them saying thank you for their clients' loyal patronage.*' This provided instant credibility for the development company, and a believable reason for these lectures being held free.

The ISP also agreed to design and host the website that would take all the enrollments, giving the personal development company accurate details on all the enrollees, as well as the business contact information for each one.

So what did the personal development company have to provide in return?

Well, the ISP requested that they make a series of appearances at schools where they are launching a new campaign. **So the deal was a win-win for both sides**, it cost the ISP company <u>nothing</u> as sending the e-mail invites was free, and the personal development company had **more than 5,000 people sign-up** in exchange for giving up some of their time to make appearances at schools designated by the ISP!

So what is it exactly that makes this endorsement strategy so effective?

Creating Astounding Goodwill And Trust With Clients

Essentially an endorsement is just obtaining approval from another person, or business, concerning what you are doing—in this case, it would be the approval of the products and services you are providing those who need your help.

Now the power of using endorsements, to gain an instant increase in new leads, lies in the fact that many businesses have already established a **high-quality reputation** for delivering impressive solutions to their clients. When that business recommends their clients to look at what you also provide, their clients believe that if the business **trusts** your results…then they most likely can too.

This is what makes the endorsement strategy so much more efficient while also providing such a remarkable return on investment.

Instead of spending large sums on approaching cold prospects, who *may* be interested in what you are providing, you instead approach businesses that service the exact types of clients you **can** help—then work out an arrangement with them to provide something of value to their clients—something that reflects positively on the business endorsing it.

If this is a strategy your business could benefit from, then you might want to know…

How To Create Win-Win Endorsement Offers

The following steps are the suggested actions to take when intending to create, offer, and benefit from a strong endorsement relationship.

These steps are not '*written in stone*', so feel free to expand on them, or try various approaches until you find a process you are comfortable with, however these have worked for thousands of other business, around the world, to generate insanely profitable results. Having said that, let us start with the first step...

Step 1: The first thing you want to do is determine who your ideal prospective client would be. Look at your existing client base and identify the common traits that your long-term, more profitable clients, share with one another.

Step 2: Create a list of the various problems, pains, and frustrations with which your ideal prospects are struggling in accomplishing their desired result (*more money, better health, improved relationships, and so on.*).

Step 3: Identify a way to either provide useful information (*as educational advice*), or an **exciting** special deal on your products and services that can help eliminate some problems, pains, and frustrations identified.

Step 4: Identify potential centers of influence (COI) that have an existing relationship with the same type of ideal clients you are looking for. These might be other businesses, membership groups, associations, and even respected individuals within the community.

Step 5: Contact these potential COI businesses and let them know you have something of value that you would like to provide their clients, something that is **not** freely available to the public, that would not only help their clients solve their immediate problems, but would also strengthen the bond those clients have with the business because they helped them by *'arranging such an amazing offer'*.

You should also prepare answers in advance, for any potential questions, such as: *'why would my clients care about this?'* or *'**what's in it for me** to do this for you?'*

One potential option, to consider, is the endorsement of a valuable offer made by the COI to your clients, while it is truly an impressive offer that would provide value to their situations. But really, at the end of the day, all you need to do is…

Start Using This In Your Business Today

Remember, the biggest factor (*in determining how successful this strategy can be*) is going to be the quality of the businesses you approach to endorse you.

Look at their business practices, how they represent themselves to their clients, what general client feedback is about the business (*online reviews, and so on*) and any other elements you need to verify to ensure that they are indeed the business that you want your business to be associated with, much less endorsed by.

Other than that, it is just a matter of determining the best valuable offer to provide their clients, and going from there!

Perhaps, like the previous example, you decide to provide free seminars to their clients. Well this can be done either online through a presentation style known as a 'webinar', or it can be done off-line in a traditional speaking arrangement, but of course the biggest thing is that you **focus on providing helpful solutions** and not just a <u>flagrant</u> sales pitch to buy your products.

By providing true value, and helping your new leads obtain genuine results, they are much more inclined to want to buy additional products and services from you afterward, but you need to establish your ability to help them first without them feeling they need to risk their money, health, time, with a new business.

Here is another example showing that …

One Business Rapidly Achieved 50% Market Penetration

In this example, a recently founded Internet company had developed a cutting-edge new technology—a way of delivering fast Internet access to residential users, at a fraction of their current *'popular'* service provider.

Knowing that this was exciting new technology, the company began to establish a large sales and marketing team, then decided that the product would be so compelling that it would most likely sell itself once potential clients found out about it…

So the company began to visit local computer resellers, and computer stores, within the geographical areas they would be initially servicing. The employees within these stores—at least the ones that interact with clients regularly—loved to talk about the latest technologies, so it only made sense to *'spread a rumor'* among them about this exciting new technology that *might* be coming to their area!

Well, once the company finally did announce their technology was indeed coming to those geographical areas, the stores were more than happy to promote the faster Internet service to their existing computer-oriented clients.

After all, the employees were excited, which led to the clients becoming excited, and because the company was servicing smaller towns of roughly 300,000 people...it did not take long for word to spread around town of this new high-speed network, cheaper than the slower more expensive one used by the residents.

*So what was the 'magical' secret to getting each of these various computer stores to **enthusiastically** agree to promote this new Internet service to all their clients?*

Well, as was mentioned before, the *'magic formula'* for a successful endorsement agreement relies on two things:

1. An exciting special offer

2. An agreement that provides a benefit to the endorsing company as well

To ensure the success of this endorsement strategy, the company explained to the computer stores that this new technology would allow their clients to have a **better experience using their new computers**, and it would **save them hundreds of dollars** compared with using their current Internet provider.

In terms of how the agreement benefited the computer stores, the company provided the computer stores the ability to sell the Internet subscription service to their clients, <u>as an additional option</u> at the time of purchase, in exchange for the computer store retaining the client's first month's payment for the subscription.

This arrangement finished being worth **thousands of dollars** in additional profits for each store, profits that cost the endorsing stores nothing to promote, yet generated even more goodwill and trust with their clients as a result – a win-win!

*So what was the result of this **purely word-of-mouth** endorsement strategy?*

The company **achieved a 50% market penetration** in specific neighborhoods, and <u>the computer stores helped brand the service</u> as the **best thing** for their clients!

By helping other businesses provide additional value to their clients, you can obtain similar results for your marketing through positive word of mouth about the value your business provides clients that choose to do business with you.

If you would like help with developing an exciting offer, or identifying potential centers of influence, just **contact me at PreeminentBusinessSystems.com.** Now the next step is…

CHAPTER 3

GETTING PROSPECTS TO KNOW, LIKE AND TRUST YOU

Most businesses focus all their marketing budget, and effort, on trying to '*brand*' their company in the minds of their marketplace. However, effective '*branding*' is not bought, instead it is a by-product of a strong word-of-mouth reputation within your marketplace.

Instead of focusing on '*branding*' a business, the most successful businesses instead **focus on bonding** with their client base, truly <u>understanding their needs</u> and providing valuable solutions that reflect on this understanding of client needs.

This leads to your clients not only being happier, and remaining more loyal to your business, but can also...

Have Clients Quickly Opening Their Wallets To You

You see, once you have established your business as a familiar authority within your marketplace, an authority that can be trusted to provide correct information that helps your clients get the results they want…they are more willing to follow any buying recommendations you make to them.

They buy because **they believe you truly want to help them** get their desired results, not just make a quick sale then move on to the next client in line.

This simple strategy, of establishing yourself as a trusted authority within your marketplace, is not only powerful for generating an increase in sales, but also it can be accomplished with no additional expenses required, just the time it takes to provide helpful information for the clients.

This whole strategy can be summed up with three words… **…Sharing valuable information!**

Not just '*any*' information, the key word is it must be **valuable** to the recipient.

The reason many prospects pass on the opportunity to buy from your business can be the absence of important information to base their decision on.

Do you have **a specific solution that is exactly what the client needs**, but that they may not know exists to solve their problem?

Do the products you sell **last three times as long** compared with '*lesser quality*' products that prospects might be considering buying because of price alone?

Is there a way that your clients can **use your services to get an even better result** for what they originally intended to achieve?

Well then you need to share such valuable information with them!

This is **a HUGE leverage opportunity** that many of your competitors often just ignore, and by ignoring it, they have a big challenge ahead of them trying to compete with you once you begin to implement it within your business!

Just imagine: A potential prospect contacts your business to ask about a specific product or service you provide. You then provide them with additional information, **which they may not have**

known, that makes them realize their first choice may not have been the best selection for them—then you explain why another option might be **better suited for their exact needs**—then they buy your recommendation based on their improved understanding of what they need.

This one strategy of taking the time to educate clients, on its own, can…

…SKYROCKET your sales closing percent and generate a TON of new clients!

In fact, here is a case study of how…

One Business Increased Their Sales To $63,000,000

It is a relatively straightforward story really: an ink-company for metal-based objects realized how important it was to educate their clients once they began to ask their clients questions about what they knew concerning the company's inking process—and many of their clients replied with either **miss-informed** answers, or just complete **unawareness**, on what inking processes were used to get their results!

So the company accomplished a structured 'educational program' for new leads, and hot prospects about to make a purchasing decision.

These educational seminars began with the basics of how inks are formulated and manufactured. Then lead into chemistry, terminology and raw materials. The company would explain how ink is formulated for each individual process and what the critical attributes are, and to their surprise—they were bombarded with questions immediately following their presentations!

Almost like real-time market research, they received information on product concerns, industry complaints, product complaints, compliments—and so on!

The ink-company then established step-by-step processes and systems for measuring and mapping the needs of clients for them, eliminating any confusion on getting started, then established project management time-lines for setting objectives and deliverables...leading clients the entire way from start to execution.

So what was the result of this education-based approach to selling?

They positioned their company as the world leader for metal decorating inks supplied to all can manufacturers—and exploded sales to a jaw-dropping $63 million in sales—all by taking the time to eliminate the confusion and provide valuable information to their clients and prospects!

In fact, this strategy of 'educational selling' is one of the better ways to…

Easily Take Clients Away From Your Competition

The reason this is so effective is because you are not only providing free information to prospects and clients, that truly makes your ability to achieve your desired result much easier, simpler, faster, and so on, but you are also **eliminating any possible confusion or objections**, in their minds, that might cause them to hesitate in making a buying decision.

Oh, and of course I cannot forget the fact that if your competition is NOT taking the time to educate prospects, to provide them with *valuable* information, and your business *does* take the time…that it just makes the stimulating of **word-of-mouth excitement** surrounding **YOUR** business much more effective—*true branding*.

By identifying key concerns, or confusion, within your marketplace, and providing free resources to help your market get over such hurdles, you are establishing your business as the 'go-to business' for help—you are building a '*brand*' reputation as a business that wants to help your clients get the best results.

Now you might be wondering…

How To Accomplish This Powerful Strategy For Increased Sales

As mentioned for the previous strategy, the following steps are not '*written in stone*', feel free to experiment with your approach so you achieve the best results for your business' specific target market.

Having said that, here are the steps that have been used by **thousands of successful businesses** to *easily* accomplish 'educational selling' into their sales funnel:

Step 1: Create a list of the objections a prospect might have to making a purchase, the frequently asked questions prospects have about the products and services you sell, and finally a list of questions prospects <u>SHOULD</u> *ask before* buying to <u>avoid</u> any post-purchase disappointment or negative experiences.

Step 2: Create educational resources that address each issue, help the prospect to achieve their desired result, or helps clients obtain better results from any recent purchase(s) they have made.

Step 3: Should a prospect choose not to make a purchase, proceed to follow-up with them providing the above information, such as answers to common questions, and resources that could help them solve their current problems, pains, and frustrations

Step 4: Once you establish regular communication with prospects, and your existing clients, continue to invite them to contact your business should they have any questions or concerns. This not only helps address any reluctance prospects have to buying, but can also allow you to communicate **empathetically** with clients.

Step 5: The final step is to measure the feedback from prospects and clients.

Now that you know how to accomplish the strategy, it is time to....

Easily Explode Your Sales Using This Strategy

The key to success with this strategy is to focus on the needs of your target market—then do everything you can to help them get what they need.

If prospects contact your business, to inquire about a solution you provide, give them as much information as possible so they can make the best buying decision.

Should a prospect choose **not** to make a purchase during this first contact, make it a point to *follow-up* with them, providing high-quality information and resources that can help them solve their current problem or achieve their desired result.

And do not think you must wait for prospects to approach your business before you educate them—*as the following case study shows*—educating your market with your marketing materials can be a powerful strategy for attracting new clients.

In this example, a small computer sales and service firm from Beit Shemesh, Israel, was placing regular advertisements in the weekly newsletter with two or three other computer companies…

But the advertisements of all three companies were almost the same: each showed a computer system, described its power and features, then gave a price. This is a mistake made by many businesses as seen in places like the Yellow Pages, Flyers, and so on.

Realizing this, the computer company decided to take a radical new approach to their advertising and began *to educate* their prospects. They began to run advertisements with such headlines as 'What is Memory?' and 'What is a Hard Drive?' with 'What Kind of Scanner Should I Buy?' and 'What is a Motherboard?' and so on.

So what were the results of their new educational selling approach?

By changing their advertisements the company could not only **start charging more** for their products and services, but they also took themselves out of the '*price war*' with competitors by projecting an image of <u>caring for their clients</u>.

Prospects buying solely on price would still go to the competition, but the company <u>was not</u> concerned, as **they did not want** '*price shoppers*'.

However they found that prospects are now approaching their business thinking of the company as a business that **takes the time to explain** all the various options in a language they can understand. These prospects now knew on a gut level that if they called the computer company they would get efficient and caring service.

Had the computer company just promised '*great service*' in a typical business advertisement format, they would not have developed the trust and credibility they now have.

In fact, one of their competitors went out of business, and the others have continued to advertise their systems in the same '*me too*' way, but the computer company has since **continued to increase their sales** using JUST educational selling <u>without</u> even featuring computers in their advertisements at all.

You could easily accomplish such a marketing strategy into your business using a variety of free resources such as online videos, follow-up e-mails with prospects, creating an 'information section' within your company website, and so on.

The result is likely to be the same: your business can experience significantly **improved positioning as a trusted authority resource** within your marketplace.

If you have any questions, comments, or concerns, about getting educational selling working within your marketing process, just **contact me at PreeminentBusinessSystems.com.**

Another benefit of using educational selling is that it can…

CHAPTER 4

GET CLIENTS EXCITED TO BUY OVER AND OVER AGAIN

One of the most profitable things your business can do to quickly increase sales is to offer additional solutions to your existing clients that can help them!

In fact it can allow you to…

Rapidly Increase Your Sales With No Additional Expense

It is true! This one tactic not only allows you to eliminate costly marketing expenses by trying to promote new products and services to *cold prospects*, but also converts at a much higher rate because clients already know and trust your business.

Did you know, typically, it costs **FIVE TIMES** as much for a business to sell to a new client as it does to convince an existing client to make an additional purchase?

Now you can understand why providing additional solutions to your clients is not only more profitable, but also more time efficient as well!

In fact, it is possible to double, triple, and even quadruple the amount of each sale you make just by offering another '*must-have*' solution at the same time a client makes a purchase.

You might have seen examples of this strategy in your day-to-day activities. Even a large corporation like McDonald's, believe it or not, ***doubled* their worldwide profits** just by having employees say: '*Would you like fries with that?*'

Of course this '*upselling*' strategy can also be accomplished during the follow-up communication where you **educate** your clients about using additional solutions.

And if you do not happen to have additional solutions to offer, that is not a problem, because you can see in the following example how one company has been able to…

Generate A Consistent 28% Increase In Sales Without Any Risk

A multimedia company, that specialized in doing complete video productions for a variety of corporate and industrial clients, realized that despite clients spending tens of thousands of dollars to have their videos produced…they had nothing else to offer their clients once the client's project had finished.

However, they noticed that following the completion of client projects, their clients would approach nearby duplication facilities to have copies made for distribution to their customers, employees, or whomever. This ranged anywhere from a few dozen to several thousand video copies being ordered by their clients at these facilities.

Realizing that they were missing a profitable piece of the '*production pie*', the company approached what they found to be a friendly—and more important: honest—video duplication (only) facility with whom they could negotiate a good business deal for low prices on mass duplication projects.

So what was the result?

Well, once they established the agreement with the duplicator, they could offer duplication as a back-end service to their current, and future clients, which has **resulted in a consistent 28% increase in sales for the past TEN years**—with the *duplicator doing the work* and the production company just picking up the orders and delivering them to their clients—**providing a 50% profit margin** solution directly to the multimedia company's bottom line!

And this was accomplished by just providing what clients had already shown they needed to purchase anyway…and done without requiring the multimedia company to risk capital money on investing in their duplication machines.

An impressive ROI, which can be instantly accomplished with irresistible offers that can…

Make Your Clients Happily Buy Whatever You Offer Them

The reason they happily buy is that you are offering them valuable solutions that they can benefit from. These are solutions that they might have been intending to buy anyway…so you are **making it convenient to buy** the solution from you instead of another business.

This not only allows **them to save time** by not having to run around, *price shop*, research who the best provider of those products and solutions are, but can also keep them more loyal to your business without being '*tempted*' by outside competition—and of course there is the increased client lifetime value as well!

The secret to making this strategy effective is that the additional products and services you recommend **must be relevant** to the *original* desired end-result the client was looking for to begin with: *increasing the value you are providing!*

For example: Someone intending to buy a new suit for a coming event may also benefit from having a new dress shirt and tie to go with it…of course, because they have such impressive looking new clothes it only makes sense for them to also be interested in having a fresh pair of new dress shoes, and probably a new belt to match those new shoes, and as an added service the shoes could be polished, and so on.

You can probably see the pattern here: find valuable ways to offer additional solutions for your client's pains, problems, frustrations, or just general desires.

Of course to truly benefit from this strategy you need…

The Three Steps Behind This Profitable Selling Strategy

In its basic form, here are the simple steps for creating a profitable back-end selling system to increase your business' sales:

Step 1: Create a list of all your business' current products and services that are sold (or could be sold) to your clients.

Step 2: Identify which items, within the above list, complement other items within that list that are typically initial purchases made by one of your business' clients.

Step 3: Implement an 'upselling' system into your sales process, so when a client orders 'Solution A', from your business, they are presented with an opportunity to buy 'Solution B', which works well **with** 'Solution A' to create a better result, and experience, for the client's desired goal.

An easy, effective, and proven way for increasing sales!

All that is needed now is for you to…

Use This Strategy To Multiply Your Profits

Here are some '*getting started*' ideas for how you can begin to accomplish this strategy into the various sales processes within your business:

Instead of selling all your products and services separately, begin to package them together, with a small discount, as an incentive for clients to buy more.

Other ideas you can use for your business include…

Starting to suggest related solutions at the time of a client's purchase, then follow-up with those clients to see how their experience has been with the solutions they bought, and offer them additional related solutions then as well.

Another opportunity, for when clients make a purchase, is the opportunity to turn them into 'regular' clients by encouraging them to sign up for a 'VIP club' (of some sort) as an incentive for them to get hot deals on future purchases and receive '*VIP updates*' that entice them to buy your products and services more frequently.

Finally, if you happen to be a newer business, or just do not have any additional solutions to offer clients apart from your principal product or service, you can refer them to another business and charge a referral fee to get a piece of the profit.

Just remember to focus on helping clients get what they need and you can also profit.

Also be sure your interactions with clients, while offering additional solutions, do not come across as a 'salesperson', but as a genuine desire to **HELP your clients** achieve their desired result with the fewest challenges.

Here is an example of how…

One Business Generated An 855.88% Increase in Sales

In this example, a trade show and event planning service was using a variety of direct mail marketing methods to develop leads, and they managed to develop a list of seventy-eight 'hot prospects' from one mailing, closing thirty-four of them on a 'trial rental exhibit' at a low cost of just $400—an initial sales revenue of $13,600.

Now, instead, of being satisfied with **just** this initial sales profit, they decided to…

…Implement a back-end strategy **to increase those sales** as much as possible!

So what did they do?

Well, immediately after a new client invested into one of the trial rental exhibits, they were placed into a follow-up sequence of various **educational** direct mail pieces, telemarketing follow-up calls, and personal sales calls for a *'deluxe'* custom rental package valued at an average price of $5,000 per rental.

What was the result of this educational follow-up series?

Of the thirty-four trial clients, ten of them decided to order the deluxe version—**providing additional revenue of $50,000** for the event planning company...

...But they did not stop there!

The company then provided more information on the benefits they provide, and offered the ten deluxe clients an upgrade option to a 'full custom exhibit'—*at $40,000 each*—which two out of the ten deluxe clients bought...**a further increase in revenue of $80,000!**

The initial front-end sales for the company was only $13,600, but thanks to using the strategy of providing additional solutions, they could add $130,000 to their total sales for the event—at hardly any additional expense!

If you are not sure exactly what additional solutions to provide your clients, the simplest thing to do is just ask them what **they** would like to see provided!

Asking for feedback not only provides your business with the most accurate research possible, but also shows your clients you value their opinion, which further strengthens and extends their loyalty to you business! And as a result...

…You are able to outlast, *outsell*, and **<u>outperform</u>** your business' competitors!

And of course, should you need any help in this area, please do not hesitate to contact me by going to **PreeminentBusinessSystems.com** or by e-mail at **Merle@PreeminentBusinessSystems.com** so I can answer any questions, comments, or concerns you have with developing and accomplishing this powerful strategy for your business' marketing process.

With that said, here is…

CHAPTER 5

HOW TO GET THE MOST OUT OF THIS BOOK

First, congratulations on finishing this book, you now have a powerful three-part system for completely dominating your marketing quickly and effectively.

One thing to keep in mind is that all three strategies work well when applied together, and that their combined affect on your business only exponentially increases the results on your sales numbers—so do not restrict yourself to just one!

Another important thing to remember is that you should accomplish these strategies in small test runs, measure the results, then scale their implementation into other areas of your marketing from there.

Doing small test runs helps minimize any risk, while allowing your team to get comfortable with the strategies being used at the same time.

But no matter what strategy you start with, or whether you prefer to test in larger amounts instead of smaller samples, **the most important thing is that you act with these strategies** to get that astounding jump over your competition as the business in the examples within this book have already done.

To ensure you maximize as much of your business' potential sales growth as possible, you can also take advantage of our...

MARKETING ANALYSIS
CONSULTATION

Contact me today and we can schedule a meeting where we can sit down with your business to discuss where your business is today, the amount of **growth desired for your business**, and what the business is doing to achieve such growth.

I can then analyze your current marketing efforts to identify ways your business can quickly—and more effectively—increase its sales soon.

Also **if you know of other business owners who could benefit** from the proven strategies within this book, <u>feel free to pass this book along to them</u>, and have them **call me if I can be of any help to them** as well!

I **thank you** for taking the time to read this book, and look forward to working with your business soon to further increase your marketing results!

Sincerely,

Merle Liske

Merle@PreeminentBusinessSystems.com

101-5101 50 Avenue
Suite 710
Leduc, AB   T9E 0B9
CANADA